GW00870181

POETRAITURE

Bill McKnight has lived most of his life in Braehill, North Belfast. Tiger's Bay is not too far away and Cavehill is just around the corner. Poetraiture is his second poetry collection.

This paperback edition first published in 2017
All rights reserved

© Bill McKnight, 2017

Bill McKnight is hereby identified as the author of this work in
accordance with Section 77 of the Copyright, Designs and
Patents Act 1988.

Subject to statutory exception and to the provisions of relevant
collective licensing agreements, no reproduction of any part
may take place without the written permission of the author.

ISBN: 978-1-5485-3375-5

2

To the Arts and Disability Forum (ADF) whose generous grant
has helped make Poetraiture a reality.

Contents

Foreword

It has been a huge privilege for over twenty years to have
walked parts of the road with Bill McKnight on his
ongoing journey of healing from mental illness. This, his
second volume of poetry, captures some of the insights he
has garnered over the years, and does so in language that is
startlingly simple and deeply provocative, yet very hard to
set aside.

Mental illness may still carry something of a stigma in
some parts of our society, but this volume will
undoubtedly help those struggling with mental illness to
realise afresh that they have gifts and talents that need to
flower for the well-being of us all. Even more importantly,
these poems will compel those of us who do not have such
struggles to understand that we have much to learn from
those who do. In particular, Bill's poems point out the
need not to be squeezed into accepting values for everyday
living simply because so many others embrace them in our
increasingly consumerist and 'me first' society.

Inside this book you will find humour, satire, observation
and deep reflection. And some wonderful 'one liners' well
worth remembering. Enjoy and appreciate both the writer
and his work!

                    Very Rev Dr Norman Hamilton OBE
                    2016

Acknowledgements

Copycats, (Design; Copy; Print) 537 Antrim Road, Belfast

Mr Michael Harrison (Hewitt & Gilpin, Solicitors, Belfast)

Introduction

During my research into creative mental health recovery, I discovered Bill's first collection 'Loud Silence' (2012), which illuminates his personal experience of stigmatisation and negative social attitudes to people with mental health struggles. 'Loud Silence' intrigued me and I have been fortunate in getting to know Bill and cite his work over the past couple of years; doubly fortunate now in being offered the opportunity to write the introduction to his second collection. 'Poetraiture' takes Bill's talent to a new level, especially the way in which he captures complex experiences and insights with deceptively brief prose yet an incredibly rich lexicon.

This new collection resonates with some of 'Loud Silence's' original themes of stigma, suffering and recovery, for instance in 'Depression i and ii', 'Fear' and 'Psychiatric admission'. Yet there is, too, a clear expansion of the poet's attention and repertoire. As a series of condensed philosophical essays almost, we hear musings on the paradoxes of modernity and human disconnection in 'Sound and vision', 'History lesson' and 'The Clown'; on spirituality in 'Funny peculiar', 'Stillness' and 'Prayer'; and on the charming colloquial humour of 'Bingo wings', and 'The Kitchen shop' (Tiger's Bay 1960's).

The poems strike me as mining a similar vein to another Ulster poet, Louis MacNiece, whose sense of the world being 'incorrigibly plural' is aptly reflected in Bill's 'Poetraiture'. At one and the same time, these poems are personal and universal; unsettling and uplifting; food for thought and sparkling with gut-derived irony and humour.

Seamus Heaney, citing Basho, claimed that poetry is truth. 'Poetraiture' is a candid work, told with searing honesty as well as being refreshingly fun. To be returned to again and again, and each time to be struck by a different theme, a joke or one of the numerous delightful puns, 'Poetraiture' is a valuable addition to literature, both in terms of human insight and as a collection of poems in and of their time, place and person. It is, indeed, a portrait in words, as well as a unique piece of literature which will, I am certain, inspire many people, now and for years to come.

Roberta McDonnell PhD
2016

POETRAITURE

Progress?

Strawberry jam.

Traffic jam.

Paper jam.

2060

We're modern!

Isn't it fantastic?

Faces and banking

have all gone plastic.

Macavity's gone legal

In Frisco the old cats are crazy.

In New York the young cats are cool.

In the International Bank,

let's be frank,

it's the cutest cats who rule.

At the end of the day

they laugh and they say,

"Your money's away!"

Macavity's a fat cat.

Fancy that!

Sound and vision

Higher than snowy mountain peaks an eagle soars.

By Alpine sunny fountains ibex drink.

Through undergrowth a python slithers;

while out on the dales a lamb is born.

A hedgehog huddles under leaves.

In cold river waters trout swim.

Upstream salmon leap;

deep underground a rabbit feeds her young.

Mist is settling over the lough where midges swarm.

The sun is setting and the still night air

echoes to the blackbird's song.

And on a sofa a man is slumped;

one eye half-closed,

half-watching T.V.

Junk Food

Corrie.

Eastenders.

Emmerdale.

Neighbours.

Friends...

A diet of soaps.

X factor

Pop music.

Pop idol.

Pop corn!

Sir Alexander Fleming (2016)

"There is an

accelerating egocentrism

flourishing in

this culture!"

On parenting teenagers

"Are the dishes washed, or

are our wishes dashed?"

Ménage à trois?

The coiffured wife,

dripping in jewellery.

The sun-tanned hubby,

dripping in dollars.

The attentive waiter,

dripping in sincerity.

She gives a wink

and gets a nod.

He gives a tip

and gets a grin.

Oh! what a threesome

to be in.

Sailor town blues

Now Gertrude had a tattoo

on her upper arm, oh! yeah.

Gertrude had a tattoo

on her upper arm.

It boasted, 'Dream-boat Lillie

pulled by tugboat Sam'.

Now Gertrude's name was Lillie

and tugboat Sam her man.

Gertrude married Billy,

but Lillie thinks of tugboat

when she can.

Drinkin' thinkin'

Genevieve's an alcoholic.

She longs for a figure

like a slimline tonic.

Bingo wings

The weekend's come

and bingo's looming.

Granny's thoughts

have turned to grooming.

Her roots,

her tips,

her fringe –

enough said.

Bingo has gone

to granny's head!

Tom

Tom, Tom, the piper's son,

stole a pig and away he run;

the pig was eat,

and Tom was beat,

and Tom went howling

down the street.

Tom, Tom, the piper's son

took his case

to the Court of Human Rights

and won!

The clown

He smiles through his pain.

He's addicted to craic cocaine!

Rat-a-tat-tat

Giving information to a gossip

is like giving ammunition to a gunman.

Obesity

Paunch and Judy.

Once upon a time?

'Virgin' means wholesome?

For many, 'virgin' means -

a store,

a train,

a plane,

a shame,

or simply fair game.

Political correctness

Love-child.

Is this term

an illegitimate

use of language?

Good ol' days
(Before Thatcher, Blair and the global market)

"Manager, manager,

where are your staff,

for the time is not yet three?"

"They're down in the smoke room

having a puff

and enjoying a cup o' tea."

Globalisation

coal,

gas,

oil,

human:

resources.

Cross channel business talk

Parlez-vous franchise?

Highway robbery?

Marks & Expensives!

Nero's blessings

Health

for wealth.

Intelligence

for status, rank and reputation.

Talent

for success and fame.

The West's on fire

and Ziggy played guitar.

Eternal debt?

Ever, ever

on the

never, never.

Food for thought

'I want' and 'I wish'

are the fish

on the marketing man's dish.

'Bigger' and 'better'

are the batter

on the marketing man's platter.

Victor Frankenstein – revisited

Victor Frankenstein's

an advertiser now.

And 'artificial need'

is the monster he's created.

Play for sale

'All's swell that sells well!'

The Advertisers

The Ads men.

What are they like?

They promise you

a ride on a magic carpet

by pulling the rug

from under your feet!

Consumers

Connie and Walt are dead.

Why did they die?

Why did they live?

Marketing revival!

Christian books

to grace your bookshelf.

Depression (i)

How I used to sing

of forty shades of green.

Now all I have to say

is forty shades of grey.

Depression (ii)

Depression weighs me down in chains.

I am not Houdini.

Psychiatric admission

Dread.
Bed.
Meds.

Coke.
Smoke.
Joke.

Ill.
Pill.
Through the mill.

CD.
TV.
ECT.

TLC?
Professionals treat patients?
But people need people.

Fear

Fear is not the spider.

Fear is what's inside yer!

A romantic meal for two
(or just desserts!)

I dotted every i and crossed every t,

anxiously explaining my mental history.

(If she knows me, will she love me?)

But she voted with her feet -

a rather hasty retreat, all before the sweet.

Heavens above!

Whatever happened to her appetite for love?

Miss X showed no remorse.

And there was no second course!

Exercise – good for your mood.

Keeping fit at 51?

I think I'll take the car out for a run.

Fudge

Truth … iness.

Little Britain

The corner shop of honest doubt

is being forced out of the street

by the retail giant

of wholesale unbelief.

Doubting Thomas

"God's good.

(Touch wood)."

A modern god

Microwaveable bolognese!

Saves time.

Saves money.

Saves effort.

Self-service

couldn't be simpler.

Little Miss Lies

Miss – demeanour.

Miss – represents.

Miss – informs.

Miss – ery.

Funny peculiar

Whatever happened

to the fun

in fundamentalism?

The scientist and the Christian

He investigates;
he believes.

He reasons;
he accepts.

He is rational;
he is intuitive.

He is factual;
he is spiritual.

He proves;
he hopes.

He thinks;
he loves.

He is a father;
he is a brother.

A Christian and a scientist.

Proverb

Loneliness gnaws at the bones;

jealousy rots them.

Prayer

Help me please God.

Help me please God.

God, please help me.

Get real!

It is perfectly normal

to be imperfect.

Calvin who?

Whilst clergy quarrel over Calvin,

whole communities are dying

for Calvin Klein.

Worry

Worry is a 'me' thing.

If

If money's not the answer,

what's the question?

Grace

Rest amidst stress.

Frank SINatra

"I did it my way."

Shadow boxing?

Cowardice is a hard thing

to fight.

The Lord is my Shepherd

Lord, I know not

what today holds.

Hold me.

Sovereign God

God works in time.

God works on time.

Soul

On a grey day in a suburb

church bells peal

for a widow, newly departed.

Her body was lowered

into a watery grave,

but the sun shone through clouds

like an anthem.

Downtown, shoppers set the tone,

and 'jingle bells' is what the tills are ringing.

Xmas 2015

Christmas cakes.

And tray bakes.

Simply divine!

Christmas 2015

No room in the …

fridge.

Bling Crosby

I'm dreamin' of a white …

wrist-watch.

Christmas surfeit

'tis the season to be jolly,

Tral-la-la-la-la-la-la-la-sigh.

Chain reaction

I remember

the swings in the park.

I remember

the swings chained in the park

on Sundays.

I remember

my hurt in the park on Sundays

in Belfast

in the swinging sixties.

The Kitchen shop (Tiger's Bay 1960's)

Davy Rowan's bacon slicer was a great machine.

Its rotating blade cut tongue and cheese and ham.

And so far as I'm aware,

Davy never lost a finger to the guarded blade.

There was time for talk.

Courtesy was very much the currency of the day.

And though the queue moved slowly

one felt one had been served.

"Have a nice day," was a million miles away.

Davy and his family had a nobler way

with the customers in Tiger's Bay.

Ghost stories

A candle burning

in one corner of the room

sets the night aflame,

casting intricate shadows

of objects otherwise mundane.

Fingers become forests;

faces ghostly and aglow.

And stories more mysterious grow

as embers in the fire burn low.

At the midnight hour

sleep has lost its power

and children learn of tales

from long ago …

The Limestone Road

Inner city streets and shops
and mill lie derelict.
Like a mouthful of rotten teeth
In a grim-faced interface.
Houses shut-up. Shops shut-down.
Barely a stone's throw from the town.
Long gone the limestone route
from Cavehill to the shore.
No more familiar sounds
of family life and work –
community life-blood sucked out
by sectarian strife and the passage of time.
Now flags flap in rhyme,
demarcating border lines.
The hymn for this scene is, "Abide with me."
Sung to the tune of
'ten dozen stinking pigeons'.

The Twelfth

There are those

who beat their drums

for kicks.

I prefer

chicken drumsticks.

History lesson

Caesar salad

and

Burger King.

Modern history

in the making!

Poet?

My name is Bill McKnight.

I couldn't write a poem

to save my life.

Stillness

Mental illness knows no borders

and crosses all divides.

She is rude, crude, or polite and sophisticated.

Her abodes are thoroughly complicated.

Her's the silent cry for help, or vicious screams.

Mental illness is a terrible mistress

and seldom what she seems.

Friend, fear God, not mental illness.

God's grace gives the longed-for stillness.

Postscript

Having only met Bill very recently, I was worried that I might be the wrong person to read and comment on his work. But perhaps that is the point of good literature: it has the ability to bring people closely together in a very short amount of time. It also has a unique way of showing us that people are not so very different from one another after all.

Bill's work is refreshingly uncomfortable. His keenly observant poems, concisely expressed, accomplish a very rare thing: they are a subtle yet powerful invitation for us to pause and reflect on ourselves and the world we inhabit. They are both introspective and obtrusive, entering the imagination and taking root in a quiet corner of the mind, to be enjoyed in the moment, or to be revisited time and again to serve as a sounding board for further introspection. These poems are not polite comments. They are instead vibrant expressions of everyday life that demand we take note of them. They are not easily forgotten. Bill's poems succeed at turning the mirror inward, shedding light on the most fascinating and complex subject of all: the reader himself.

Chloe Ferrone
2016

44855169R00049

Printed in Poland
by Amazon Fulfillment
Poland Sp. z o.o., Wrocław